Antwerp Research Institute for the Arts, University of Antwerp
AP University of Applied Sciences and Arts Antwerp

The Immersive Performance of Visual Poetry. The Result of a Quest for a Renewed Literary-immersive Art Experience where the Audience, as Receiver/Viewer/Reader, is Immersed Together in an Immersive Poetic Experience of Image, Sound, Language, and Spatial Experiences.

The Immersive Performance Poetry of Philip Meersman: A Multidimensional Exploration

Thesis submitted for the degree of doctor in the Arts at the University of Antwerp to be defended by Philip MEERSMAN

Supervisor UAntwerp: prof. dr. Kevin Absillis
Supervisor KASKA-AP: Dr. Johan Pas

The PhD researcher and supervisor(s) declare that the PhD research was conducted according to the principles of scientific integrity, as mentioned in the general PhD regulations and charter for PhD researchers of UAntwerp and the integrity charter for PhD researchers and supervisors affiliated with the University of Antwerp.

In preparing this article, I employed AI-assisted language editing to refine clarity and style as recommended by the reviewers and create the abstract with keywords. Furthermore, I experimented with AI-supported article formatting for *Text and Performance Quarterly* and to generate a consistent bibliographic layout. Although I explored the possibility of linking each poem from the *Oceanus Refertus* book & booklet to the relevant chapters through AI, I ultimately chose not to use those suggestions. All video materials referenced in the chapters were selected and curated manually; I created the final list myself, based on my own judgment and the abundance of available work. The AI-models used were ChatGPT, Copilot & Perplexity.

ABSTRACT

This essay reflects on my work as an immersive poet, performer, and interdisciplinary artist who collaborates with visual artists, musicians, designers, and technologists to stage poetry beyond the page. I frame poetry as a union of five interdependent modalities—written, oral, read, aural, and performative—and argue for planetaria (rather than headset VR) as the ideal environment for collective literary immersion. Drawing on Cubo-Futurist ZAUM, avant-garde art & poetry, Flemish visual-poetry lineages (Van Ostaijen, De Vree, Ramon, Fierens), and theories of speech act, voice, and participation, I theorize a poetics in which book, body, and dome co-perform. A narratological analysis of my In the Future series (fabula vs. sujet) shows how repetition, looped time, and image generate immersive dramaturgy. The essay further discusses poetry of resistance, visual scenography, the politics of reception in a post-truth condition, and ethical questions around AI authorship, documentation, and access. Case studies from Oceanus Refertus: Microplastic Paradise on a Slip of Paper and performance video documentation ground these reflections.

Keywords: visual poetry; immersive performance; planetarium; fabula & sujet; ZAUM; Flemish visual-poetry; post-truth; AI authorship; Flemish avant-garde

TABLE OF CONTENT

ACKNOWLEDGEMENTS

I would like to express my profound gratitude to all those who have guided, supported, and inspired this doctoral research.

My deepest thanks go first to **dr. Johan Pas**, whose early enthusiasm in 2016–2017 set the first ripple across the water, a disturbance that grew into the larger current carrying this PhD forward. I remain equally indebted to the initial supervisory constellation of **prof. dr. Luc Van den Dries** and **prof. dr. Hans Vandevoorde**, whose early encouragement helped shape the estuary in which this project first took form. My sincere thanks extend to **prof. dr. Kevin Absillis**, whose sharp critical tide and unfailing generosity deepened the conceptual seabed of this research. I am grateful to **prof. dr. Kurt Vanhoutte**, President of the Supervisory Committee, for navigating the larger oceanic dramaturgies of performance and media, and to **prof. dr. Annick Schramme**, co-supervisor and President of the Jury, whose insight into cultural policy and artistic ecosystems widened the coastline of this work. My warm thanks also go to **dr. Thomas Crombez**, who guided my trajectory from ArchiVolt to MAXlab—two essential landfalls in this voyage.

My gratitude reaches like a tide toward **Gert Smet** and **Rodrigo Alvarez**, whose stewardship at the Royal Observatory of Belgium and the Planetarium of Brussels opened the dome as both a night sky and a pelagic deep. Under their care, poetry could drift freely between constellations and currents, crossing the brackish threshold where cosmos meets ocean. Their unwavering support became a vital lifeline — a rope anchored to both horizon and seabed.

Warm thanks go to **Janna Beck**, a steady lighthouse across shifting fogs, whose drawing, projection, and guidance helped chart new passages through tidal silt and stellar dust. To **Luna Moraga Garcia** whose visual and material sensibilities shaped many of this project's reefs, islets, and floating architectures, and **Nikola Meersman**, the first shipmate indicating visual clues and guide to the sky, I am deeply grateful.

The Urban Travel Machines (UTM) consortium formed a rich archipelago: drifting islands of poets, visual artists, coders, and dramaturgs stretching from the Baltic to the Atlantic, from alpine ridges to African high plains. Instead of naming each island individually, I thank **the entire UTM archipelago**—a flotilla whose combined momentum made this research swell, crest, and break open beneath the domes where sky and sea invert.

The collective behind **Drawing Resilient Futures**, together with the project **Frietje Wabisabi**, shaped wide tidal flats where drawing, performance, and speculative world-making converged. Their work brought new sediment, new textures, new micro-landscapes to this research. Meanwhile, the immersive collective behind **VAXX.ON.AIR**, supported by MAXlab and CREATIE, created a resonant dune-cave—a tidal breathing chamber where sound, breath, and neural waveforms flowed like subterranean brine, giving rise to new forms of embodied poetic practice.

I honour with care the memory of several guiding lights now beyond the horizon. **Prof. dr. Hans De Wolf**, whose mentorship shaped my bachelor's and master's trajectory, remains a deep intellectual anchorage. The late **Wim Henderickx**, whose presence in VAXX.ON.AIR added emotional depth like the undertow beneath a calm surface, leaves a resonance still audible in each sonic experiment. And **Jean-Pierre Van Rumste**, co-founder and experimental musician of Artiestencollectief JA!, whose daring explorations pushed open tidal gates, continues to inspire the boundary-crossing ethos at the heart of this project. Their contributions endure like distant constellations and quiet beacons—guiding the way even beyond their earthly horizon.

My thanks extend also to all collaborators of **#Framed Live, Artiestencollectief JA!, DAstrugistenDA, Cro§in'X, the Jean Demey Trio, Koala**, and especially **Mario Vandermeulen**, who first opened the breakwater and the wider sea rush in, like **Lieven Vercauteren**, a multitude of quay walls. Even those who placed reefs, breakwaters, and glass ceilings along the route taught me to read the current differently—every obstruction becoming a new shore to chart.
Finally, my deepest love and gratitude go to my children **Eva, Kalina, and Nikola**, and to **Rozalina Petrova**, whose presence has been both anchor and tide, peninsula and horizon, the quiet bays where I return and the winds that push the boat onward. They remain the islets of calm amidst vast seas and the constant constellations by which this voyage finds its meaning.

INTRODUCTION: REWRITING THE EDGES OF POETRY

I do not consider poetry confined to language or to a static literary form; it is a multi-dimensional presence—linguistic, visual, sonic, spatial, social, political. Each poem is a **score** for voice and space as much as text. Performing in museums, theatres, squares, protest sites, and under the planetarium dome has shown me that the printed line is only an invitation to activation.

My guiding question remains: how can poetry become a lived, sensory, spatial experience? Collaboration—with graphic designers, musicians, XR developers, and academic partners—has been my laboratory for exploring poetry as sound, space, body, and event.

Like Magritte's La trahison des images, my poems resist representational certainty. "Ceci n'est pas une pipe" warns against easy referentiality; a poem is not what it says but **what it provokes**. My background in art sciences and archaeology trained me to read stratigraphies of meaning—layers, traces, erasures—that now shape my method: a **union of five forms** [1] (written, oral, read, aural, performative) that operate simultaneously.

In my doctoral research, *The immersive performance of visual poetry. The result of a quest for a renewed literary-immersive art experience where the audience, as receiver/viewer/reader, is immersed together in an immersive poetic experience of image, sound, language, and spatial experiences*, I explored how visual poetry, once fixed to the typographic plane, can migrate into **vocal, sonic, and immersive** forms. My poetry books trace this evolution: *This Is Belgian Chocolate* (2014) gathers multilingual, satirical, geopolitically charged performance poems; *There Is Blue Somewhere* (2020) adopts a travel-catalogue typography inflected with ecological themes; *Het Omstandereffect* (2024) assembles a destabilized media archive; and *Oceanus Refertus: Microplastic Paradise on a Slip of Paper* (2025) consisting three volumes, existing as a classic visual performance book, a visual performance booklet and a unique one off live dome performance, and is a poetic cartography of the Anthropocene that fuses visual and verbal language to expose humanity's entanglement with oceanic pollution, translating ecological data, mourning and collective guilt into an immersive aesthetic of fragmentation, colour, and sound.

I uphold the Flemish dictum that poetry is "**de allerindividueelste expressie van de allerindividueelste emotie,**" yet I stage that individuality **with others**—technicians, readers, audiences —inside a shared semiotic (image–sound–performance–spatial) field.

This ongoing negotiation between tradition and innovation also shapes my own stance as both artist and researcher. My dual background makes me acutely aware of the need to **balance passionate engagement with critical self-reflection.** My position is not one of detached observation, nor of unqualified advocacy. Instead, I strive to **inhabit a space of productive tension**—acknowledging the limitations of my own methods and the provisional nature of my claims. For example, while I argue for the transformative potential of immersive poetry, I also recognize that its effects are contingent, variable, and sometimes unpredictable. This meta-reflection is essential: it prevents the work from lapsing into dogma and opens space for dialogue, doubt, and revision. **I invite readers and audiences** to join me in **questioning** not only **the content of the poetry, but the frameworks through which it is produced and received.**[2]
To further contextualize these artistic choices, it is essential to reflect on the contemporary relevance—and limitations—of avant-garde strategies in today's digital and participatory landscape, since my work is deeply rooted in the historical avant-garde—Cubo-Futurism, Dada, Constructivism, Surrealism, Expressionism and the Flemish experimental literary, musical and artistic tradition.

However, I am conscious that directly transposing these strategies into today's artistic landscape is neither straightforward nor always effective. **The digital era has fundamentally transformed the conditions of reception, participation, and authorship.** For example, the collaborative ethos of the Russian Futurists finds new resonance in online co-creation, yet the materiality of their typographic experiments – as well as those by Van Ostayen – is challenged by the fluidity of digital text, graphic novels, emoji and stickers, the latter two being boosted through the current fast communication tools as gimmicky forms of self-expression. What content is concerned in my own practice, attempts to evoke the shock of estrangement (ostranenie) sometimes falter in a hyper-mediated environment where audiences are accustomed to rapid, fragmented stimuli. This tension prompts me to on the one hand seek for a kind of rollercoaster of emotions in my performances and to also continually interrogate which avant-garde principles remain vital, which require adaptation, and which may be obsolete. My (immersive) performances thus become **laboratories for testing the relevance of historical strategies**—sometimes succeeding, sometimes failing, but always foregrounding the question: how can the spirit of artistic rupture be meaningfully reactivated in the present? I will elaborate on different aspects further in this essay.

Relevant poems:

- Poetry will not be performed
- In the Future
- In the Future N Future
- app
- Enter a New Era
- Disclaimer

Relevant performance

- Excerpt 1 of the performance of Artiestencollectief JA! at the poetry festival "Teranova 2006" (Annex B, 1)
- XVI Rosario International Poetry Festival (Argentina) (Annex B, 8)
- Battlefield Poetry, a Manifesto (Annex B, 13)

---

[1] "Poetry is a unity which consists of a quintet of manifestations. These manifestations or appearances are two external appearances, namely the "written form" and the "spoken" or "oral form", two internal appearances, namely the "read form" (wRitten form) and the "heard form" or "aural form" and an overlapping appearance both internal and external, namely the "performance", which expresses and supports the iconicity of language parts through co-speech gestures and prosody and is presented within a spatial and temporal framework interpreted in the context of creation and perception." Meersman (2015) This definition is elaborated based on one of Roubaud (2009, p. 18-20) : "What is important here, is the fact that (t)he external aspects of a poem are interpersonal. They are transmissible to practically anyone who speaks and reads the language in which a given poem is composed.
The internal aspects are personal. They are in the mind of the reader-listener; essentially nontransmissible from one person to another; they are always in movement within memory: movement of images, of thoughts. Ultimately, the external written form is idle, but not the internal mental page that constitutes the wRitten form.
There is no poem without reading and (i)f (a poem) has not entered a single mind, a poem does not yet exist. So a reader or "audience" is essential for a poem to exist and like with art, the audience is essential in the process of finalising the poem."
I personally believe that there is one aspect more that needs to be added to Roubaud's definition, namely: "performance". "Performance" for me is part of the external aspects and can be defined as "these verbal and non-verbal forms of expression and posture, which are not strictly oral or 'spoken'".
When a baby splutters, babbles or lets out a cry of pain after a fall, or sweet smile...We are familiar with the meta-meaning of baby's babbling and know what the flipping of the middle finger means and can interpret a person's conspiratorial wink or hands forming a heart shape an the gestures of a police officer directing traffic.
Within communication sciences this is identified this as forms of multimodal communication.
This form of communication develops before speech and is recognized as communication by the environment in which one grows up or lives.
These co-speech gestures can be hand movements, facial expressions, postures, portraying what is in a text (or not!), the intonation of the voice, the movement and positioning of the performer with regard to the viewer-reader-listener, but also elements that have to do with the performer's appearance, such a dress, use of colour and make-up, perfume (or lack thereof), etc. All these co-speech gestures direct the interpretation of what is communicated verbally, visually or auditorily. In other words, our interpretation of the 'score' is guided by the 'performance'. (See Meersman 2015 and 2024)

[2] These interactions and questions have mostly been not-formally documented and are present in mail-exchanges, after-movies of festivals and events, not recorded discussions and conversations between peers and with audiences, but also have been physical at festivals where empty beer cans were thrown at me, or audiences are queueing up to ask for selfies.

THE POETIC ASPECT: POLYPHONIC ARCHITECTURE OF TEXTUALITIES

A poem is never singular: it reverberates. I write **for the echo, the memory, the body, the visual, the glitch**, constructing associative networks of rhythm, gesture memory, and multilingual (and multidisciplinary) interference. Magritte's play between word and image becomes a productive *trahison*: semantic closure constantly offered and withdrawn.

Cubo-Futurist **ZAUM** (Khlebnikov & Kruchenykh) privileges phonetic energy over syntax; I echo this transrational method in neologisms and sonic collisions that foreground texture. Chion's (1994) concept of "reduced listening" names this attention to sound's materiality. Typography and white space simulate time, erosion, and forgetting—Mallarmé's blank space meets bureaucratic estrangement. Multilingual absurdities fracture syntax, producing a Brechtian *Verfremdungseffekt.* I expect not only an emotional, but also a mental and referencial connection of my audiences, a willingness to also jump into the rabbithole which leads to a new kind of (dystopian?) Oz, acknowledging that *we are not in poetry, anymore.*

Context, material and the layout itself is designed meaning. The page functions as archaeological site—Derrida's archive where preservation and erasure coexist. I have noticed in my writing practice the way I construct my poetry, the materials and techniques used as well as the location where I work on the poetry, have a profound impact on the way they emerge and are finalised, hence I started to turn my poems into sculptural, location-bound works of art, dating them, just as visual artists do. I also added – referencing to exhibition labels - a marker of the creation location and the used writing techniques and materials to my poems. In this way also to invite the audience to start their own excavation processes, not just within the layers of my work, but also to add their layers of contextual meaning and interpretation as I discussed already in my master paper (Meersman, 2015), refering to Duchamp's theorectical frameworks, which is elaborated further.

My collaboration with Luna Moraga Garcia on *Oceanus Refertus* made this visible: syntactic flow breaks, page structures carry rhythm, and colour logic encodes ecological decay. Luna decided to not put these labels – like in *There Is Blue Somewhere* and *Het Omstandereffect* at the end of a chapter or the book, but to provoke the reader with those labels before even starting the chapter, to influence the reading of the work and to therefore use nudging as a technique to steer a certain audience interpretation of the poem itself, similar to the introduction a musician or stage performer would do before the next song/poem/piece on stage or like an introductory tekst in an exhibition room to contextualize. "The use of the indefinite article "an"/"a" in the audience's reaction/interpretation is a deliberate choice. The society in which the recipient is living, their surroundings, their own previously acquired knowledge, and (shared) history all contribute to their (an) emotional response. This reaction can align with my goal in creating the visual context of the poem, but it can also be a completely opposite or unexpected emotional reaction. See further

Relevant poem(s):

- Pilgrimage
- World Flamenco
- Currents
- Once Upon a Time
- Praline
- LII and the Bleeding from the Margins
- Seven Clarions Call
- Churning Poetry

Relevant performance(s):

- Cro§in'X, Cross-disciplinary Set (Annex B, 14)
- Boetedoening procession (Annex B, 12)
- Collaboration with Mario Salis: Si j'étais (Annex B, 2)
- TryOutDef Poetry Performance, M HKA Antwerp (Annex B, 5)
- Impro with Jean Demey Trio, Sint-Niklaas (Annex B, 16)
- Collaboration with Matete Motsoaledi (Annex B, 19)

THE PERFORMATIVE ASPECT: EMBODIED MEANING, VOICE AS TEXT, SPECTATOR COMPLETION

Performance is not an extension of poetry but its **embodiment**. Following Austin (1962), every utterance is an act; with Butler (1993), each reading reiterates identity; with Dolar (2006), the voice exceeds meaning. I treat breath, intonation, and gesture as semantic generators.

Influenced by Artaud (1958), Kaprow (1993), Schechner (2002) and Fischer-Lichte (2008), **I try to build co-creative spaces where spectators complete the poem.** As McNeill (1992) argues, **gesture is part of language**; Eco (1989) and Jauss (1982) see the artwork as "open." **Meaning emerges through bodily interaction**. My performances often invite movement, murmur, or call-and-response, integrating audience sound into the score. On the contrary to my page poetry, the use of introductary or binding texts are strictly limited – during "classical" longer performances – to what is purposeful for nudging the audience towards a certain emotional spectrum to create an "emotional rollercoaster" model towards catharsis.

Technological and collaborative experiments have not always yielded predictable results, prompting critical reflection on the relationship between theory and practice. Some performances have been exemplatory and a joy to **do where all the elements came together** and even for me **as performer space, time and performance felt as one** like with *Artiestencollectief JA!* (video 1), *DAstrugistenDA at BXLBRAVO* (video 6), *DAstrugistenDA Interview with fragments of different parts of the Boxing Ring I & II Performance Series* (video 10), *Boetedoening (procession)* (video 12), *Cro§in'X Cross-disciplinary Set* (video 14), *Frietje Wabisabi* (video 22), *VAXX.ON.AIR* (video 23) or *Ohrid, North Macedonia* (video 30).

The systematic coupling of theory and practice in my work is not always seamless. Sometimes **geopolitical, historic and/or cultural contexts or differences interfere** with how I try to make the audience "complete" the poem through the previously described nudging technique and audience collaboration. Other performances—such as early attempts at audience-driven improvisation—revealed the unpredictability of co-authorship and the difficulty of sustaining collective attention.
In one instance, a participatory sound-poem dissolved into cacophony, prompting a reconsideration of the balance between structure and openness. **These failures are instructive**: they highlight the **need for adaptive methodologies** and the value of feedback from collaborators and audiences.

I have begun to incorporate post-performance reflections, interviews, and audience surveys into my process, using them to refine both theoretical models and practical approaches. By foregrounding these lessons, I aim to demystify the creative process and underscore the importance of iterative, dialogic development.

Relevant poems:

- No Nightingales in Nicosia
- Walls
- Schadenfreude
- Currents
- Concerto for Vacuum Cleaner and Voice
- Tiger Leap
- Melope(e)(n) with Hugo
- DD

Relevant performances:

- Collaboration with Mario Salis: Si j'étais (Annex B, 2)
- Ghent Portus Ganda Festival (Annex B, 3)
- TryOutDef Poetry Performance, M HKA Antwerp (Annex B, 5)
- XVI Rosario International Poetry Festival (Argentina) (Annex B, 8)
- Breda BUTFF Festival (Annex B, 9)
- Breda BUTFF Festival (Annex B, 10)
- Boetedoening procession (Annex B, 12)
- Drawing Resilient Future (Annex B, 26)
- Impro with Jean Demey Trio, Sint-Niklaas (Annex B, 16)

THE IMMERSIVE ASPECT: POETIC SPACE AND EXTENDED REALITY

Immersion is both artistic and ethical: it dissolves distance. Planetaria serve as collective theatres of language. Unlike headset VR, which isolates, the dome maintains co-presence. Spatialized sound (Blesser & Salter 2007), projection, and live caption-as-image unite into a continuous dramaturgy (Gorman 2017).

In 'Méditerranée, zo blauw," the phonemes *bl* (drowning) and *auw* (pain) are projected as ripples; the audience floats in sonic water. This echoes Cubo-Futurist simultaneity and constructivist page dynamics translated into light and movement. The space itself becomes co-performer. The visual atmosphere has been redesigned from the idea to use ASR (speech-to-text) captioning adding visual texture and errors generating ZAUM-like slippages to underwater imagery and life jackets to **create an visual-auditory meta-imagery.**

The **integration of artificial intelligence** into my practice introduced a **new set of ethical and creative challenges**. Where in the midst of my research period I was in awe of this technology and decided to create adapted imagery via AI, it became with every attempt clear that the emotional layer couldn't be added to what seemed to be creating a clearly artificial layer of surreal imagery. In the last year I left this path and returned to the planetarium library and earlier imagary used in collaboration with the Brussels planetarium which works on its own, together with own digital creations made of found footage, personal pictures and film archives as well as freely available library footage.

I felt **I couldn't respond to the raised urgent questions about authorship, bias, and archival integrity by integrating artificial intelligence into my poetic practice.** AI-driven speech-to-text and generative tools can indeed expand the sonic and visual vocabulary of performance, they can also introduce new forms of error, exclusion, and opacity. Sometimes these ASR system's misrecognition of multilingual utterances could produce unexpected poetic fragments—transforming technological failure into creative opportunity, but the use of AI and ASR systems also expose the limitations of current models through showcasing that they privilege dominant languages often erasing minority voices, which I elaborate upon later in this essay. Within the current geopolitical situation the risk that AI models are programmed to become even more culturally biassed, reducing their original library of input through sensorship. This could result in not being able anymore to create anything but Italian Brainrot guided by an encyclopedia of directive prompts. Although new tools and models promise deeper immersion, they fail to recreate the look and feel of immersed reality, because of current lack of physical sensory inputs. And even if they would be able to recreate a true immersive VR reality in the future, this would demand a renewed ethical vigilance: How to ensure transparency, inclusivity, and human agency in a landscape increasingly shaped by a certain type of consumarist addictive algorithmic mediation and state sponsored sensorship?

Relevant poems:

- Mediterranee, zo blauw
- Mare Nostrum
- Water Washes These Sins Away
- Schrödinger's Fuge
- Swimming Lessons: A Hedging Strategy
- A Spiral Halts
- Oceanus refertus microplastic

Relevant performances:

- Urban Travel Machines (Annex B, 31)
- Performance Poetry Biennial (Annex B, 30)
- Drawing Resilient Future (Annex B, 26)
- VAXX.ON.AIR (Annex B, 23)

THE PUBLIC ASPECT: PARTICIPATORY CARTOGRAPHIES AND POETIC URBANISM

Public engagement is an integral part of my artistic practice. Whether in site-specific performances or street interventions, I conceive the city as a poetic interface. Kwon (2002) and Bishop (2012) inform this approach; Jauss (1982) underscores situated meaning.

During the pandemic, I mapped linguistic memories of Brussels neighbourhoods through co-created texts installed on trees, fences and walls. Earlier projects like the *Portus Ganda Fireworks Poem* (2006) and the *BxlBravo Guantanamo Protest* (2008) demonstrated **poetry as public ritual and political gesture** (see Videos 3 & 6). In the poetry installation project *Darfour* (Antwerp, KAFKA, 2000) passers-by helped paint textual surfaces with sand and pigment, performing memory and witness.

Across continents—from Tartu to Durban, Rosario to Trivandrum—I have tried **through performances to turn venues into archives of trauma and resilience** and to work towards the effect that each **public iteration becomes a cartographic act linking poetry, movement, and community.**

The embodied reciprocity of these public encounters finds scientific resonance in recent neuroaesthetic research. Contemporary studies of poetry's effect on the brain reveal that **collective listening activates emotional and reward circuits** akin to those stimulated by music. Futher this essay situates this physiological evidence within the broader framework of immersive language performance.

Relevant poems:

- Walls
- Pilgrimage
- Of Ancient Books and Maps, the Quest and the Sea
- Mare Nostrum
- Terre Cible
- The Entry of Brussels by Annie Cordy
- A County in a Terraced House
- Society

Relevant performances:

- Poetry Africa (Durban) - Poetry Picnic in the Courtyard (Annex B, 24)
- Poetry Africa (Durban) - Connect the Poets (Annex B, 25)
- Drawing Resilient Future (Annex B, 26)
- Breda BUTFF Festival (Annex B, 9)
- Breda BUTFF Festival (Annex B, 10)
- Boetedoening procession (Annex B, 12)
- Collaboration with Matete Motsoaledi (Annex B, 19)
- Ohrid, North Macedonia (Annex B, 30)

THE PUBLICATION ASPECT: THE BOOK AS INTERFACE AND PERFORMATIVE OBJECT

I want to build books as architectures. With Drucker (1995) and Tschichold (1928), typography is semantic; with Ingold (2007), writing is movement of thought; with Magritte, language's treachery becomes productive. Layout, paper, and colour form syntax. Readers literally **perform** pages by turning or rotating them.

In *Oceanus Refertus*, typographic erosion and colour codes allegorize plastic pollution and colonial afterlives. The repeated "orange bobs" motif transforms print into kinetic memorial.

The act of reading a book is performative. With my travels and through working with graphic designers I have tried to integrate a gaming phenomenon called "**Easter eggs**", to motivate the reader of my work to become actor-performer-researcher. **Nudge** this person to **search further and deeper, not just for meaning, but also for the hidden, coded messages** referring to not just the so called "elite" art scene, but also to popular culture, geopolitical events or natural phenomenas etc.

Relevant poems:

- Of Ancient Books and Maps, the Quest and the Sea
- Mare Nostrum
- Mediterranee, zo blauw
- No Nightingales in Nicosia

Relevant performances:

- Breda BUTFF Festival (Annex B, 9)

THE NEUROAESTHETICS AND SEMIOTICS OF LANGUAGE PERFORMANCE

Building on the discussion of materiality, where typographic design functioned as a performative interface, this section explores how linguistic and visual stimuli operate on a neurophysiological level to produce pleasure, empathy, and immersion.

Poetry, Pleasure, and the Brain

Recent **neuroscientific research** has confirmed empirically what poets have long intuited: **poetry engages and rewards the human brain as intensely as music.**[1] Studies conducted by Wassiliwizky et al. (2017) at the Max Planck Institute for Empirical Aesthetics and by Zeman et al. (2013) using functional MRI show that poetry activates neural circuits associated with musical pleasure, emotion, and memory. When participants encountered self-selected poems that resonated emotionally, their brains "lit up" in areas tied to the reward system—specifically the nucleus accumbens and amygdala—mirroring responses normally triggered by beloved music or profound aesthetic experience.

These findings establish a **scientific basis for the affective power of poetry**: the rhythmic, sonic, and semantic interplay of verse stimulates both cognitive and emotional pathways. For my own immersive practice, this research underscores that **language performance is an embodied neurological event**—a multisensory process of resonance, anticipation, and release.[2] In dome settings, the audience's collective breath and pulse synchronize with vocal rhythm, producing potentially measurable pleasure responses that align with what the Max Planck team describes as "chills" or *frisson*. **Poetry here could function as a neural choreography of empathy, bridging art and physiology.**

Colour as a Semiotic and Emotional Dimension

Alongside sound and rhythm, colour functions as a vital semiotic layer within visual poetry. As Francis Edeline (2012) observes, "colour is a dimension of the visual sign, together with form and texture," giving poets "an additional channel of meaning, simultaneous to the linguistic one and conveyed directly by colour without the help of words." This principle governs the design of *Oceanus Refertus*, where tonal gradations serve as autonomous signifier. Not just within the designs, but equally within the wording itself: blue evokes depth and mourning; orange—echoing life vests—marks peril and survival; black indicates environmental loss.[3] Edeline's theory validates my intuitive use of colour emotional syntax. The chromatic field thus extends poetic rhythm beyond sound into a visual vibration perceived somatically by the audience. The interesting part here is that the reception of the nudging intentions could be completely the opposite, which was the reason why the CoLLoC-project couldn't reach a conclusive end result, it pointed towards the fact that **the emotional syntax of color could be as diverse as the existing languages and cultures** (https://informationisbeautiful.net/visualizations/colours-in-cultures/).

Situating performance poetry within 'Language Performance"

The concept of **language performance** situates poetry as an art of action rather than description—the *doing* of language. Drawing from both linguistic and performative paradigms, it encompasses the **artful, intentional manipulation of linguistic elements**—syntax, rhythm, tone, texture—to communicate, evoke, and provoke. It integrates the **spoken, written,** and **visual** modalities into a continuum of expression that foregrounds the materiality of language itself.

In my own work, I try to include the following into my '‘language performance":

- **Artful use of linguistic form:** deploying repetition, phonetic interference, and multilingual collisions to generate sonic texture.
- **Spoken presence:** rhythm and intonation shape emotional contagion; the microphone and dome acoustics transform voice into spatial sculpture.
- **Written and visual composition:** typography and layout as performative gestures that dictate reading speed and emotional cadence.
- **Narrative and storytelling:** the transformation of geopolitical, ecological, and personal narratives into performative ritual.
- **Emotional communication:** voice and gesture channel empathy through physical vibration and breath.
- **Audience engagement:** co-creation through call-and-response, gaze, and movement—what I call '‘collective prosody."
- **Interdisciplinary expansion:** fusion with sound design, live drawing, and projection to create poly-artistic events.
- **Temporal and spatial awareness:** pacing, silence, and spatial orientation determine perception and meaning.
- **Iterative reflection:** each performance acts as research—language tested through embodied feedback.

This framework wants to position language performance as both an aesthetic and cognitive practice—a dialogue between the neurophysiological, the emotional, and the social.

The Critical Reflection of Practice: Time, Space, and Presence

For the reflective documentation and conservation of performance (Lawson 2023; Tate 2022), every activation of a language artwork must identify its **constants** and **variables**. In my practice, these parameters would be the following:

- **Time:** each poem has a core temporal architecture—loops, pauses, and rhythmic recurrence—that may stretch or contract according to acoustic feedback. Duration becomes dramaturgy (anticipating the analysis of temporal non-linearity).
- **Space:** the dome or chosen site dictates acoustics, sightlines, and audience disposition; every space becomes both instrument and stage.
- **Body:** gesture, stance, and breath are semantic tools; the performer's physiology translates emotion into rhythm.
- **Presence:** the artist's visibility and vulnerability are ethical conditions; authenticity and fragility convey truth in a post-truth era.
- **Audience:** spectators evolve into participants; their movement and gaze alter sound dispersion and projection focus, producing an ever-shifting co-authored environment.
- **Flux and constancy:** voice, text, and projection could be seen as constant; tempo, improvisation, and audience interaction are the true variables.

This matrix—time, space, body, presence, audience—constitutes the grammar of my **immersive language performance**. It ensures that each iteration of a poem remains faithful to its conceptual essence while embracing situational change, echoing *the autopoietic feedback loop* described by Fischer-Lichte (2008).[4] This looping is used also extensively during collaborative works such as *Frietje Wabisabi* (Video 22) and *VAXX.ON.AIR* (Video 23) where improvisation with poetry, music and drawing is making the poet, artists and musicians work as active-reactive tools, turning them into interlocutors of each other via intense sessions of active listening and interactive creation.

The rhythmic loops and durational elasticity analyzed here foreshadow the manipulations of fabula and sujet detailed further, demonstrating how temporal perception is both a cognitive and affective construct.

Embodied Evaluation: The Artist and the Public

The questions guiding my reflective process parallel those proposed in performance-conservation discourse:

- How is time structured in relation to meaning?
- How does spatial configuration influence interpretation?
- What is the expressive function of the body?
- How does artist presence recalibrate audience attention?
- What modes of participation emerge—static witnessing, active co-creation, or spontaneous improvisation?

In *Poetry Will Not Be Performed and In the Future N Future*, for instance, temporal loops invite collective breathing; in *Boetedoening*, spatial procession transforms onlookers into participants; in my *UTM-performances*, the colour spectrum layered with vocal frequency, transformed observation into kinesthetic empathy. Each event thus becomes an experiment in **reciprocal embodiment** confirming that the emotions poetry generate - observed by Wassiliwizky et al.- arise from shared neural and emotional resonance.

Visual Rhetoric and Cognitive Engagement

Research on visual rhetoric (Huhmann & Albinsson 2018) provides a complementary analytical lens: rhetorical figures in images and text stimulate interpretation through tension and resolution. In visual poetry, this operates through simultaneity: the viewer reads and sees, decodes and feels. My hybrid typographic-projectional works employ visual tropes such as metaphor *(image = idea)* and *metonymy (colour = emotion)* to produce cognitive emotions akin to the neural "aha" response described by Ramachandran & Hirstein (1999). This convergence of semiotics and neuroaesthetics also shows the central claim that **performance poetry engages the whole sensorium**—vision, audition, motion, emotion—making the performance venue a site of embodied cognition.

Toward a Neuro-Performative Poetics

The integration of neuroaesthetic insight, colour semiotics, and performance methodology supports strongly the position that immersive poetry operates simultaneously on cognitive, emotional, and social registers. It transforms linguistic data into *affective environments*. In this light, the poet is not only an author but also a designer of neural experiences: modulating rhythm, hue, and gesture to elicit emotion, reflection, and ethical awareness. The planetarium's hemispheric space, enveloping sound, and chromatic projection translate the internal structures of language into shared sensory phenomena—*a living brain writ large.*

These findings on neural resonance, chromatic emotion, and embodied temporality establish a perceptual groundwork for the narrative experiments where poetic time itself becomes immersive architecture.

Relevant poems:

- Beak
- Sea Soap Shower
- Dancing on Dead Dolphins
- Bloodsuckers on a Rooftop Terrace
- Where Did All The Poets Go
- There Are More Africa's For Us In A Few Million Years

Relevant performances:

- Guantanamo Protest, BxlBravo Festival (Annex B, 6)
- Battlefield Poetry, a Manifesto (Annex B, 13)
- VAXX.ON.AIR (Annex B, 23)
- Marathon TV Host Appearance (Annex B, 20)

---

1 Within the study of Wassiliwizky et al. (2017) it is shown that *"recited poetry can act as a powerful stimulus for eliciting peak emotional responses, including chills and objectively measurable goosebumps that engage the primary reward circuitry. Importantly, while these responses to poetry are largely analogous to those found for music"*

Allmost all studies on neurobiology of aesthetic experience or emotional responses have been made about music. There are studies on poetry and grief, poetry as therapy and/or medicine, but it would be interesting to have more studies on the neurobiology of aesthetic experiences and the different brain reactions related to reading versus hearing poetry and in relation to experiencing music like the cited one and Margulis, E. H., Levine, W. H., Simchy-Gross, R., & Kroger, C. (2017). Expressive intent, ambiguity, and aesthetic experiences of music and poetry. PloS one, 12(7), e0179145. https://doi.org/10.1371/journal.pone.0179145

2 The lack of comprehensive neurobiological studies on audience reactions to experimental, co-creative, and interactive performances and the way these (can) create tension in audiences, as the historic avant-gardes did and do by deliberately provoking; the tactics used by performance or slam poets by shouting or using their voice in an unpleasant way; would be beneficent for the future of poetry-off-the-page studies. The positive emotional reactions can and must be seen as an archetype of the emotional reaction defined by it's indefinite article, positive or negative for that matter.

3 Within an international context colors can have other (political or religious) co-notations, which I have experienced during a performance series in India as well as on the African continent. See further

4 The exchange between performers and spectators is self-creating and mutually conditioning. This exchange forms a dynamic, self-perpetuating system where actions and reactions constantly (re-)shape the event in real-time, generating meaning and materiality through their shared presence, rhythmic interaction, and unpredictable responses, moving beyond static art objects to experience performance as an emergent, transformative "event".

TEMPORAL STRUCTURES IN IMMERSIVE POETICS: *FABULA*, *SUJET*, AND POETIC NON-LINEARITY

Russian Formalism distinguishes **fabula**—the chronological chain of events—from **sujet**, the presentation or arrangement (Shklovsky 1917; Tomashevsky 1925; Chatman 1978; Genette 1980). My immersive works tries to purposely unhook them. *In the In the Future* cycle the *fabula* is linear—a promised temporality ("there will be time ...")—while the *sujet* is cyclical and orbital: refrains loop, captions orbit, temporal logic folds back on itself. In the book *Oceanus Refertus* itself, elements of linearity and repetition are visually and/or textually re-interpreted, they pop up at different places within the book, triggering the reader's memory as well as questioning the place, space and meaning of the used words within and throughout the surrounding contexts.

Projections in the dome circle like satelites or planetary rings; whilst pauses and micro-silences elongate perception. Each recurrence re-signifies expectation, turning time into a shared environment. The audience occupies the **present tense of delay**—a lived form of anachrony. The use of self composed beats via a beatmaking program live or pre-recorded assists in this shared time-environment. The integration of visual visual, aural, oral, written or wRitten imagery works both as a shared and/or distorted reality with time as the shared environment.

The repetition in the poetry series In *the Future* shows how the pacing of spoken lines enact narratological defamiliarization (*ostranenie*). Barthes's (1977) "writerly text" becomes literally writerly: spectators assemble *fabula* from fragmented sujet streams by turning heads and bodies within the dome.

The manipulation of time through *fabula* and *sujet* reveals that poetic temporality is inseparable from ethical perception. The next section extends this inquiry to the socio-political sphere, examining how repetition, disinformation, and affective rhythm operate within the post-truth condition, and how poetic form can resist these manipulations through defamiliarization and ecological empathy.

Relevant poems:

- In the Future
- In the Future II
- In the Future, N Future
- There is Only an End
- A Spiral Halts II
- Until The Day Dies

Relevant performances:

- Nachtelijke Optocht from Paul van Ostaijen part of Bezette Stad (Annex B, 7)
- Breda BUTFF Festival (Annex B, 9)
- Collaboration with Matete Motsoaledi (Annex B, 19)
- Frietje Wabisabi (Annex B, 22)
- VAXX.ON.AIR (Annex B, 23)
- Ohrid, North Macedonia (Annex B, 30)

POETICS OF ECOLOGICAL AND POLITICAL RESISTANCE: THE BYSTANDER, THE WITNESS, THE DISRUPTION

Building on the temporal and narrative analyses previously elaborated, this section shifts from perceptual structure to ethical praxis. If time in poetry can be bent, repeated, and dislocated, it can also be weaponized—a reality that the post-truth era has made painfully clear.

My poetry has, from its inception, been inseparable from activism — pacifism, ecological grief, and anti-authoritarian critique. **The "bystander effect" becomes a poetic architecture:** hesitation as structure, repetition as ethical stammer. Lines fracture, voices echo, and subjects dissolve, performing the paralysis that defines our era's moral and communicative crises. I attempt to interrogate disinformation and the affective logics of "alternative facts." Following Chomsky (2016), Zuboff (2019), Latour (2017), and Foucault (1977), I strive to treat language as a battlefield where power and resistance are enacted through syntax, rhythm, and silence.

Performances such as *Battlefield Poetry, a Manifesto* literalize this: the poet as citizen-combatant, deploying the voice as weapon and refuge. In *No Nightingales in Nicosia* the karaoke-bar setting frames empathy as mediated spectacle, collapsing entertainment and atrocity. *Water Washes These Sins Away* erodes bureaucratic moral certainty through iterative legal phrasing; *Words Can Never Be Virgin* exposes linguistic violation and the impossibility of innocence. *Walls* stages inclusion and exclusion through interactive buttons — a choreography of border politics where in the dome performance I have incorporated an AI-generated child's voice to create affective disorientation: a technological ventriloquism that oscillates between empathy and unease. The *Currents* suite riffs on Duke Ellington's *Caravan*, mapping global trauma by aligning psychiatric conditions with art movements, deepening perceptual instability. Each work re-enacts the collision of truth and distortion that defines the twenty-first-century sensorium.

Post-Truth and the Poetics of Disorientation

As defined by Oxford Languages (2016) and elaborated in the Oxford Research Encyclopedia of Communication (2018), ***post-truth* describes a socio-cultural condition in which "objective facts are less influential in shaping public opinion than appeals to emotion and personal belief."** Scholars identify its roots in the erosion of epistemic trust (ScienceDirect, 2020), the weaponization of affect (INSS 2021), and the algorithmic mediation of reality (ECFR 2022). **Post-truth is not the absence of truth but the *strategic inflation of feeling* over evidence.** In such a climate, poetry—anchored in ambiguity yet committed to sincerity—offers a counter-practice: it makes perception itself strange, forcing recognition through *defamiliarization.*

Drawing from Viktor Shklovsky's (1917) theory of ostranenie—"to make the stone stony"—**defamiliarization in my work ventures to function both formally and politically.** As Gilliam (2023) reminds us, **the goal of defamiliarization is to *slow perception* so that habitual seeing and hearing are disrupted.** In *Oceanus Refertus*, the repetition of syntactic units ("orange bobs orange bobs...") compels the reader to confront the mechanical rhythm of waves filled with dispersed life jackets, drowned bodies and the habituation of people to atrocitic imagery via waves filled with dispersed life jackets, drowned bodies and the habituation of people to atrocity imagery via media saturation. In performance, this becomes sonic attrition: the audience is forced into awareness of its own desensitization. Defamiliarization thus becomes resistance—a poetic technology that re-awakens empathy where post-truth culture numbs it.

The post-truth condition also redefines the *ethics of witnessing.* Where social media produces empathy fatigue through overexposure, the poem re-introduces *temporal friction.* By layering speech, projection, and gesture, I labor to extend what Navarro Fuentes (2020) calls the "crisis of mediation" into a site of critical participation. **Rather than illustrating disinformation, my performances essay to enact it:** glitches, stammers, and conflicting visuals and tonal intonations reproduce the instability of lived information ecologies. The designing of the performance is intentend in that way so **the audience experiences disorientation not as confusion but as moral cognition**—a state of heightened attention which could be related to what Zeman et al. (2013) observed in the brain's response to emotionally charged verse.

<u>Materiality, Labels, and the Poem as Object</u>

In this context, **I consider every poem an *art object*, subject to material constraints and techniques comparable to sculpture or painting.** Just as the label beside a painting might read oil on canvas, 60 × 90 cm, each of my poems carries a similar genealogy: *written on phone screen, typed on laptop, pencil on paper.* **These notations are not trivial**; the medium determines the rhythm, lexicon, and intimacy of composition. Poems conceived on a smartphone adopt the clipped syntax of messaging; those written by hand breathe in longer, tactile cadences. Like marble versus clay, the substrate shapes gesture and texture. This material self-awareness foregrounds process as poetics and situates language performance within the wider arts discourse on medium specificity.

The practice also constitutes **an act of transparency in a post-truth world**: the label becomes a declaration of method, a small restoration of credibility in an ecosystem of hidden algorithms and deepfakes. **By naming the tools of creation, the poet reclaims authorship as ethical accountability.** In exhibition contexts—planetaria, galleries, or digital projections—these metadata-labels function as meta-poetic commentary, aligning the poem with visual-art conventions while exposing the technological and embodied labour behind every utterance.

Ecological Echo and Iteration

The *Oceanus Refertus* cycle embodies ecological resistance through its recursive structure. Thematic refrains—migration, pollution, digital saturation—recur across poems but are never identical. Like oceanic currents, they circulate and mutate. This repetition with variation mirrors the persistence of ecological crises: the same images return, slightly altered, reminding readers that **catastrophe is cyclical, not episodic.** The poem *Of Ancient Books and Maps, the Quest and the Sea* entwines environmental and mythological registers, transforming reportage into ritual. In this way, iteration functions as both aesthetic and political form guiding perception through repetition rather than assertion.

Interactive works such as *VAXX.ON.AIR* and *Drawing Resilient* Future translate ecological anxiety into improvisational collaboration, fusing affective computing (Picard 1997) with participatory ethics (Bishop 2012). Through embodied defamiliarization and declared materiality, my practice aspires that resistance in the post-truth era lies not in reclaiming certainty but in cultivating attention—a fragile, communal, and deeply human act. **Immersion intends to transform spectatorship into embodiment**; here, that transformation acquires political urgency, which than could be aligning with the neural feedback dynamics discussed above. Here poetry aspires to become a site of collective emotional reaction and re-animation: the audience's co-presence and breathing could materialize in this way a shared vulnerability. In this feedback loop, poetry does what factual discourse cannot—it re-sensitizes.

The defamiliarized language, declared materiality, and recursive thematics of my ecological works transform poetry into an ethics of attentiveness—a resistance not by assertion but by presence. These reflections should lead to **immersion itself as a moral practice: a post-textual, multisensory ethics for navigating the fractured realities of our time.**

Relevant poems:

- Water Washes These Sins Away
- Words Can Never Be Virgin
- Walls
- Currents
- Sea Soap Shower
- Taste
- Degrees
- Loneliness

Relevant performances:

- Battlefield Poetry, a Manifesto (Annex B, 13)
- Drawing Resilient Future (Annex B, 26)
- VAXX.ON.AIR (Annex B, 23)
- Nachtelijke Optocht from Paul van Ostaijen part of Bezette Stad (Annex B, 7)
- Breda BUTFF Festival (Annex B, 9)
- Breda BUTFF Festival (Annex B, 10)
- Collaboration with Matete Motsoaledi (Annex B, 19)

PLANETARIA OVER HEADSETS: CO-PRESENCE, ACCESSIBILITY, CONSERVATION

Following the ethical and political reflections, this section re-situates immersive poetry as an ethical paradigm—an embodied response to the cognitive and ecological fragmentation of the post-truth world.

Planetaria offer four interlinked advantages for live literary immersion:

1. **Co-presence and shared attention.** The dome's horizon allows collective listening—an ethics of togetherness rarely possible in VR headsets.
2. **Accessibility and safety.** No hardware barriers or motion sickness; sign language and gesture remain visible.
3. **Documentation and conservation.** Dome systems enable multi-track recording compliant with Tate's performance-documentation protocol (2022).
4. **The Cognitive Ecology of Poetic Immersion.** Multisensory binding within the brain is supportive of the multimodal notation for embodied cognition where language is experienced as a field of consciousness.

Allow me to elaborate briefly on these four points to clarify why planetaria offer a unique intersection of spatial, acoustic, and cognitive affordances for immersive literary experience, unlike the isolating nature of head-mounted virtual reality (VR) systems.

Dome environments generate what may be called an **ethics of co-presence**—a space in which voice, gesture, and collective attention converge into a single hemispheric field. The dome is both projection and shelter: a physical and symbolic horizon that allows poetry to be experienced as a shared event rather than a solitary simulation.

Co-Presence and Shared Attention

Within the dome, the 360-degree horizon functions as a **cognitive membrane** that enables distributed attention and shared embodiment. This aligns with Claire Bishop's (2006) understanding of *participatory aesthetics*, where **meaning emerges through social encounter and collective elaboration** rather than through the isolated gaze of the individual spectator. The planetarium's enveloping architecture thus reactivates the social dimension of poetry performance as a communal mode of listening and perceiving.

Projects such as *Urban Travel Machines* (2023–25) and *PoetryFest Brussels* (2014-2024) demonstrate these dynamics through immersive live projections in which animated images (pictures, video, planetarium projections, typography,...) travel along the dome's curvature, synchronised to the performer's vocal performance. This transformation of text into moving light exemplifies what Meersman (2024) defines as **visual prosody**—the rhythmic interrelation of linguistic, sonic, and spatial components structured according to Gestalt principles of perceptual organisation. In these performances, language becomes light, and prosody becomes architecture. From a neuroaesthetic perspective, collective entrainment in such environments activates **mirror-neuron systems and limbic synchrony** within temporal and pre-motor cortices (Zeki 1999; Ramachandran and Hirstein 1999). These regions mediate empathy and rhythm perception, turning the poetic event into a shared neural choreography. Thomas Hirschhorn's notion of "the public inside a brain in action" (Bishop 2006, 10) finds its literal manifestation in the planetarium dome, where the audience collectively inhabits the synaptic theatre of the poem.

Accessibility and Safety

Planetaria, unlike headset-based XR systems, afford **open, non-exclusive immersion.** They eliminate hardware barriers while maintaining visibility of gesture, motion as language, and facial expression—elements crucial for inclusive cultural access. In *The Color of Language – The Language of Color* (Meersman 2023–24), a start was made in developing a real-time speech-to-text artificial intelligence with the intention to make it part of the scenography itself with dynamic captions to operate not as mere accessibility tools but as **visual extensions of voice**, synchronised with pitch, timbre, and breath. The development needed to create an automatic transcription which becomes **a form of light poetry**, but couldn't be realized because it would take a significant investment on all fronts. The result could be a space where live text bands trace the prosodic movement of sound, where transcription errors or delays—termed *ZAUM glitches* after the Russian Futurist concept of *zaum* (transrational language)—transform semantic failure into expressive texture. This process resonates with McKenzie, Thwaites, and Hope's (2023) "careful and curious" framework for artistic evaluation, in which error and uncertainty are generative rather than defective. Accessibility thus becomes aesthetic: a multimodal field where language, light, and emotions coincide.

Documentation and Conservation

The **documentation potential** of planetaria extends far beyond traditional stage recording. Multi-channel systems—audio arrays, projection metadata, gesture tracking—enable comprehensive archiving of performance according to the Tate's *Performance Documentation and Conservation Protocol* (2022). Here, performance is defined not as an unrepeatable event but as a network of reproducible parameters that capture the performative ecology rather than a single instantiation.

Within Urban Travel Machines, each poetry event is preserved as a **polyphonic dataset** comprising a soundtrack, textual documentation and poetry transcription, projection information, and a 360° video, sometimes also pictures or video exerpts from the actual performances itself. This methodological layering aligns with McKenzie et al.'s (2023) proposal for affect-based evaluation, in which documentation itself becomes a creative and ethical act—**an archive that generates value** rather than extracting it. Consequently, immersive poetry acquires ontological resilience: instead of fossilising the performance, the archive records its relational vectors and reactivates them in future installations or scholarly reconstructions. **Documentation becomes the continuation of performance by other means.**

The Cognitive Ecology of Poetic Immersion

Neuroscientific studies confirm that poetry engages **distributed neural networks** encompassing auditory, visual, and motor cortices, as well as limbic regions associated with emotion and autobiographical memory (Obermeier et al. 2013). When rhythmic voice patterns coincide with visual motion and spatial acoustics, **cross-modal integration** in the brain could create a multisensory binding. *multisensory* binding. This process could indicate the audience's sense of being physically implicated in the poem's unfolding (see also above in earlier sections).

Meersman's (2015 & 2024) concept of poetry as score articulates this phenomenon: a poem is not solely linguistic structure but a **multimodal notation for embodied cognition**. Planetaria could materialise the metaphor of the brain as stage—hemispheric domes that mirror hemispheric thought—transforming internal mental imagery into collective, luminous performance. Within this setting, language ceases to be merely read or heard; it is **experienced as a field of consciousness** projected in light, sound, and motion.

Relevant poems:

- Mediterranee, zo blauw
- Oceanus refertus microplastic
- Zum Beispiel Die Welt
- Hiraeth

Relevant performances:

- Poetry Africa - Drawing Resilient Future (Annex B, 26)
- Urban Travel Machines - A Coruña (Annex B, 31)
- Slam MX workshop & performance, Mexico (Annex B, 17)
- Kritya International Poetry Festival (Annex B, 15)

The immersive ethics outlined above depend on transparency, attentiveness, and shared agency. The next section situates these principles within the technological horizon of artificial intelligence and speech-to-text systems, examining how post-truth estrangement, perception, and ethical responsibility can converge in the digital co-creation of poetry.

AI, SPEECH-TO-TEXT, AND POETIC RESPONSIBILITY

Artificial intelligence has entered my practice not as a neutral instrument but as a philosophical collaborator—a site where authorship, perception, and responsibility intersect. In the context of post-truth culture, AI technologies both magnify and expose the epistemic tensions between representation and reality. Drawing from Chalmers (2022), who argues in *Reality+* that **virtual worlds are not illusions but "real worlds realized by digital means,"** I regard AI environments and speech-to-text systems as co-realities: extensions of perception in which meaning is generated through code as much as through consciousness. When I try to use technological innovations in my performances, the algorithm becomes a participant whose estranging output reveals the material instability of language itself.

Following the principle of **defamiliarization** (Shklovsky 1917; Gilliam 2023), AI errors and glitched transcripts serve as deliberate acts of estrangement. They make the familiar uncanny, slowing perception and compelling both artist and audience to re-interrogate the trust placed in technological mediation. In a post-truth condition where digital tools are often vehicles of misinformation, this **re-estrangement of machine language functions as critical resistance:** it re-introduces doubt, attentiveness, and human interpretive agency. The aim is not to anthropomorphize the machine, but to reveal, through its distortions, the fragility of our own cognitive frameworks. As established earlier, **the neural emotional response to rhythm and colour relies on embodied perception.** When AI re-produces or mistranslates signals, it estranges the same affective processes, revealing both the promise and the peril of machinic mediation.

Three ethical axes orient a possible integration of AI within poetic performance:

1. **Authorship and Ontology.** Generative models can extend typographic, sonic, and spatial vocabularies, yet their products are ontologically hybrid—neither fully human nor entirely synthetic. Following Chalmers's claim that "virtual entities are as real as physical ones," each AI-assisted poem must disclose its co-creative lineage. Dataset provenance, model architecture, and curatorial intervention constitute part of the artwork's ontology and should accompany publication metadata. The fact that (co-) authorship is a controversial topic, because what source data AI is using depends on what these learning models have scraped and integrated into their models, and these models not always cite their original source material. Therefor I do not use AI to create poetic work.

2. **Bias, Accessibility, and Estrangement.** Automatic Speech Recognition (ASR) systems privilege dominant linguistic corpora; accents and minority languages are algorithmically marginalized. Incorporating such errors as aesthetic material—what I term algorithmic estrangement—requires ethical transparency.
   Archive copies and transcriptions must identify both the system's bias and the poet's corrective strategies. Defamiliarization becomes not only artistic but restorative: an attempt to make bias visible rather than

silently perpetuated. The algorithmic distortions encountered here echo the linguistic ruptures of earlier: both transform misinformation into aesthetic form, translating the rhetoric of post-truth into a performative awareness of instability. My CoLLoC (Collor of Language – Language of Color) research has shown that the current language models cannot produce a creative visual interpretation of visual or oral poetry (scripts). They are trained to recreate the standardazed words, based on the interpretation by the model of the sounds provided, and that following the dominant languages. Other models try to make psychological statistical emotional interpretations, again based on dominant linguistic and psycho-analitical data of a restricted dominant linguistic group. Therefor I decided to not broadly use AI as speech-to-text but contemplate text-to-speech models in my performantive work.

3. **Documentation and Versioning.** As **Lawson (2023)** and the *Tate Performance Documentation Guidelines* (2022) note, reproducibility in performance is an act of translation, not replication. In AI-driven work, model parameters, training data, and software versions become part of the *performance score*. Recording these elements allows future re-staging while acknowledging temporal drift—the algorithm's evolution as a new performer with each iteration. By foregrounding transparency, versioning, and algorithmic accountability, the poetics of AI advance the immersive ethics articulated above. The machine, like the poet, becomes an ethical interlocutor—a participant in what the preceding chapters have described as an ecology of attention. The use of labels to mark creation processes, tools and locations, in my work, related to common practice in visual artworks, is a first step in this process. The analysis of AI models is needed to be able to foresee the necessary documentation, but with these models lacking transparancy - as described above - this becomes problematic and hence less probable to be used in my artistic practice.

In this framework, AI is both *mirror and mimesis*: it reflects the current dominant cultural logics of post-truth while offering tools for their critique. Its mishearings, semantic ghosts, and forced straightjacket make it at this moment a problematic tool because of the lack of psychological and sociological linguistic diversity being integrated into the models. By folding machine cognition into poetic practice, I failed to show not technological transcendence but ethical clarity. The versioning and research should create an art that acknowledges its algorithms, estranges its automatisms, and reclaims human responsibility within the expanding realities of the digital.

Relevant poems:
- Words Can Never Be Virgin
- Beak

Relevant performances:
- Red River, Mozilla Hubs (Annex B, 27)
- Open Doors Red River, Two-Headed Horse (Annex B, 27)

The decision to **write and perform primarily in English** was shaped by both pragmatic and artistic considerations. While English offers **access to a global readership and facilitates international collaboration,** it also transforms the rhythm, imagery, and reception of my poetry. Comparative analysis of my Dutch and English texts reveals shifts in tone, syntax, and cultural reference—sometimes opening new possibilities, sometimes introducing loss or estrangement. **My work is indebted to** poets, musicians, visual artists and performers I have met and worked with over my career of almost 40 years on stage. I integrated styles, languages, sound, music, hardware, effects and peformance aspects from **so many inspiring artists.** But, more importantly, my work remains indebted to the **Flemish experimental tradition**, drawing on figures such as Gezelle, Van Ostaijen, Snoeck, De Vree and Ramon.[1] This lineage informs not only the visual and sonic dimensions of my poetry, but also its ethos of linguistic play and resistance. **By situating my practice at the intersection of languages and traditions, I seek to foster dialogue across boundaries—embracing both the opportunities and the challenges of transcultural poetics.**

The implications of this linguistic and cultural positioning merit further reflection, especially in relation to the Flemish experimental tradition. My transition to English followed repeated rejection in Dutch-language circuits overshadowed by lyric traditions which seemed to have been followed almost dogmatically. Encouraged by designer Mario Van der Meulen—"look at the globe and decide where you want to be heard"—I began publishing in U.S. journals and presses. *This Is Belgian Chocolate* (Three Rooms Press 2014) and *There Is Blue Somewhere* (Cyberwit 2020) established an international readership and touring network with academics, festival organisers, and poets worldwide.

These international reviews highlight—ecological resonance, digital aesthetics, postcolonial dialogue, and existential reflection and locate *There Is Blue Somewhere* at the confluence of **ecological consciousness, participatory performance, and immersive perception**—a poetic ocean where color becomes cognition, and movement, sound, and space merge

into a multisensory field. Flemish experimentalism—decending from Van Ostaijen, De Vree, Ramon, Fierens— are retaining a global resonance, or as Willard Bohn (2001)[2] argued, Flemish visual poetry influenced the international avant-garde. My work tries to reactivate that lineage through cross-media and multilingual practice. By foregrounding dialogues, I hope to situate my practice within a global poetics valuing multiplicity, negotiation, and the ongoing evolution of meaning.

Relevant poems:

- Hiraeth
- Zum Beispiel Die Welt
- The Truth Is Out There – Again
- Return
- Phoenix

Relevant performances:

- 31e Festival Internacional de Poesia de Medellin (Annex B, 21)
- Bright Brussels, Beacon of Hope (Annex B, 28)
- Nachtelijke Optocht from Paul van Ostaijen part of Bezette Stad (Annex B, 7)
- XVI Rosario International Poetry Festival (Argentina) (Annex B, 8)
- Tartu / Tallinn (Estonia) (Annex B, 11)
- Poetry Africa, Durban – Centre for Creative Arts (Annex B, 18)
- Ohrid, North Macedonia (Annex B, 30)

---

1 the influence of these Flemish experimental and avant-garde poets is clearly present in the use of onomatopoeia, alliterations, assonances and other linguistic uses of language in my work, furthermore the visual influences of those avant-garde visual poets can also be traced in my visual poetry work and has been acknowledged in different historiographic works of Dutch language visual poetry and international experimental poetry like Zieteratuur: Concrete en Visuele Poëzie, Karel ten Haaf - Uitgeverij Passage 2010; Vorm & Visie. Geschiedenis van de concrete en visuele poëzie in Nederland en Vlaanderen, Renaat Ramon - Uitgeverij Poëziecentrum 2014; the Maintenant series by Three Rooms Press; the ZAUM-almanach series by Sergej Birjukov...

2 Willard Bohn is Distinguished Professor Emeritus of French and Comparative Literature at Illinois State University, USA and author or editor of sixteen books in the fields of comparative literature, the historical avant-gardes and visual poetry (2001) and was one of my academic sparring partners during the writing of my master thesis.

My key takeaways from this essay are:

CONCLUSION: INDIVIDUATION WITHIN SOLIDARITY

If lyric poetry is, as the Flemish *Van Nu en Straks-ers* claimed, "*de allerindividueelste expressie van de allerindividueelste emotie*", then the immersive dome redefines that maxim as collective experience. The trajectory traced in this study—from the page to the planetarium—has been an inquiry into how poetry intends to embody the tension between singular voice and shared consciousness. Across the preceding sections, the fivefold framework of *written, oral, read, aural, and performative* unfolds as a multidimensional ecology in which word, body, colour, and sound act together.

At the beginning of this essay the *polyphonic architecture of textualities* situated the poem as a spatial artefact: each line a visual and sonic construction shaped by material and context. The collaborative typographic design of *Oceanus Refertus* demonstrates how language, colour, and ecological awareness fuse into a single aesthetic system. *The labels marking, pencil on paper, made in iNotes, or, typed on phone* are not paratexts but ethical declarations, linking textual composition to the transparency demanded by post-truth critique.

The essay continued to explore performance as embodiment. From *Boetedoening* and *Battlefield Poetry, a Manifesto to Poetry Will Not Be Performed*, the voice and gesture became instruments of meaning rather than vehicles of delivery. Audience participation—sometimes structured, sometimes chaotic—turned spectators into co-authors, enacting the open-work aesthetics described by Eco and Jauss. Earlier works prepared the ground for the dome performances later, where textual ideas are translated into architecture and light.

The essay continues with the immersive aspect relocating the embodiment within collective environments. *Méditerranée, zo blauw and In the Future II* exemplify how the spatialized sound, projection, and shared gaze dissolve the boundaries between performer and audience. The planetarium replaced the proscenium with a hemispheric sensorium—an ethical space of co-presence that anticipates the defence of dome over headset VR. The failure of AI-generated imagery to reproduce genuine affect underscored the necessity of human curation and the irreducible emotional layer of live performance.

By repositioning poetry as civic cartography, by labeling poems with place of creation and hence linking them to a cartographic framework. These links are even more so present with location driven performances or location based creations. From the *Guantanamo Protest Endurance Piece* over the *Portus Ganda Fireworks Poem to the Ohrid Library Performance*, public interventions mapped language onto urban and social terrain. The city became a page on which community memory was inscribed, connecting Lefebvre's spatial theory with Bishop's participatory aesthetics. These gestures re-emerged globally—in Durban, Rosario, Trivandrum—as testimony that immersive poetry can act as social ritual and ethical witness.

The essay continues with the publication itself being reframed as performance. Books operate as visual-verbal interfaces where typography, rhythm, and colour codes trigger embodied response. Neuroscientific findings by Wassiliwizky and Zeman confirm that poetry activates neural reward circuits comparable to those stimulated by music. Within dome performances, this could translate into collective neuro-affective resonance: audience and performer share physiological entrainment, a synchronization of breath and pulse that becomes the biological counterpart of poetic rhythm. Colour, as Edeline argues, could in this reasoning function as non-verbal syntax—its emotional vibration extending sound into light.

The essay also examined how time itself becomes performative through *fabula* and *sujet*. In the *In the Future series*, linear narrative (the promised future) is replaced by cyclical presentation (the eternal now). Refrains loop, captions orbit, and temporality becomes spatial. This narratological non-linearity prepares the ethical turn, where temporal distortion mirrors the informational disorientation of the post-truth condition. There, poetic iteration and defamiliarization become strategies of resistance: *Water Washes These Sins Away* converts bureaucratic diction into moral erosion, while *Words Can Never Be Virgin* dramatizes the impossibility of linguistic innocence.

Defamiliarization is further extended into ecological and political critique. Through the *Currents suite and Walls*, poetry confronted misinformation and empathy fatigue by transforming them into embodied estrangement. The AI-child's voice in *Walls* staged both technological mediation and emotional vulnerability, aligning with Shklovsky's principle that perception must be made strange to be renewed. *VAXX.ON.AIR* and *Drawing Resilient Future* advanced this strategy into improvisational collectivity, converting ecological grief into shared creation and mutual attention.

The ethical synthesis of these explorations culminate in the theorized idea that planetaria are the ideal sites for collective immersion. The dome's hemispheric architecture realises what Gorman terms *affective immediacy*: voice becomes light, gesture becomes orbit. Here, documentation and accessibility are not ancillary but constitutive, preserving both the relational and the sensory dimensions of the event. The planetarium becomes a civic brain—an architectural metaphor for shared cognition.

Immersive ethics are put in the framework of technological frontiers, where artificial intelligence, viewed through Chalmers's *Reality +*, appears not as illusion but as co-reality. It is the insisting on transparency—dataset provenance, model parameters, and algorithmic bias—which could help with a more artistic AI integration.

Finally, the essay tries to situate my evolving practice within translingual and transnational contexts. The Flemish avant-garde—Van Ostaijen, De Vree, Fierens, Ramon—remains a living current within these experiments, its visual-verbal radicalism refracted through global collaboration.

Thus, from the polyphonic page to the hemispheric dome, from corporeal chant to algorithmic glitch, my PhD-project has traced a single ethical arc: the transformation of individual utterance into collective resonance. Immersive performance poetry, as evidenced throughout my whole carreer, but here especially in the examples described and performed, reclaims the communal dimension of language in an era of fragmentation. It offers an art of listening as resistance—a practice of solidarity through attention. In the dome, the poem becomes not an object but a *condition*: a living intersection of sound, light, body, and thought. To perform is to inhabit that intersection fully, where individuality and community, technology and empathy, converge into the shared breath of the poetic real.

I agree / disagree with these conclusions

tempted in the desert
by the devil for days
wandering through dunes
in the desert for years
rainfall and flooding

behold

ANNEX A: SOURCES

Primary Creative Sources

Meersman, Philip. 2014. This Is Belgian Chocolate: Manifestations of Poetry. New York: Three Rooms Press.
———. 2020. There Is Blue Somewhere. Allahabad: Cyberwit.
———. 2023. Het Omstandereffect. Soest: Boekscout.
———. 2025. Oceanus Refertus: Microplastic Paradise on a Slip of Paper.

Other Sources

Aarseth, Espen. 1997. Cybertext: Perspectives on Ergodic Literature. Baltimore: Johns Hopkins University Press.
Artaud, Antonin, and Morgan, James O.. "The Theatre and Cruelty", The Tulane Drama Review, Vol. 2, No. 3 (May, 1958), pp. 75-77. Cambridge: Cambridge University Press.
Austin, J. L. 1962. How to Do Things with Words. Oxford: Clarendon Press.
Barthes, Roland. 1977. Image, Music, Text. London: Fontana.
Bernstein, Charles, ed. 1998. Close Listening: Poetry and the Performed Word. New York: Oxford University Press.
Bishop, Claire, ed. 2006. Participation. London: Whitechapel / Cambridge, MA: MIT Press.
Bishop, Claire. 2012. Artificial Hells: Participatory Art and the Politics of Spectatorship. London: Verso.
Blesser, Barry, and Linda-Ruth Salter. 2007. Spaces Speak, Are You Listening? Cambridge, MA: MIT Press.
Bohn, Willard. 2001. Modern Visual Poetry. Newark, DE: University of Delaware Press.
Butler, Judith. 1993. Bodies That Matter. New York: Routledge.
Butler, Judith. 2004. Precarious Life. London: Verso.
Chatman, Seymour. 1978. Story and Discourse. Ithaca, NY: Cornell University Press.
Chion, Michel. 1994. Audio-Vision: Sound on Screen. New York: Columbia University Press.
Chomsky, Noam. 2016. Who Rules the World? New York: Metropolitan Books.
Debord, Guy. 1958. "Theory of the Dérive." Internationale Situationniste 2.
Derrida, Jacques. 1996. Archive Fever. Chicago: University of Chicago Press.
Dolar, Mladen. 2006. A Voice and Nothing More. Cambridge, MA: MIT Press.
Drucker, Johanna. 1995. The Visible Word. Chicago: University of Chicago Press.
Eco, Umberto. 1989. The Open Work. Cambridge, MA: Harvard University Press.
Edeline, F. (2012). The Use of Colour in Visual Poetry. Óbuda University e-Bulletin, 3(1), 285–299.
European Council on Foreign Relations (ECFR). 2022. "How to Avoid a Post-Truth World."
ECFR Commentary. https://ecfr.eu/article/commentary _ how _ to _ avoid _ a _ post _ truth _ world/.
Fischer-Lichte, Erika. 2008. The Transformative Power of Performance. London: Routledge.
Foucault, Michel. 1977. Discipline and Punish. New York: Vintage.

Genette, Gérard. 1980. Narrative Discourse. Ithaca, NY: Cornell University Press.
Gilliam Writers Group. 2023. "Defamiliarization: The Art of Making Strange." The Gilliam Writers Group Blog. https://www.gilliamwritersgroup.com/blog/defamiliarization-the-art-of-making-strange.
Ginsberg, Allen. 1956. Howl and Other Poems. San Francisco: City Lights.
Gorman, David. 2017. Immersive Theatres. London: Palgrave.
Hayles, N. Katherine. 2002. Writing Machines. Cambridge, MA: MIT Press.
Huhmann, B., & Albinsson, P. (2018). Assessing the Usefulness of Taxonomies of Visual Rhetorical Figures. Journal of Current Issues & Research in Advertising, 40(1), 1–25.
Ihde, Don. 2007. Listening and Voice. Albany: SUNY Press.
Ingold, Tim. 2007. Lines: A Brief History. London: Routledge.
Institute for National Security Studies (INSS). 2021. "The Philosophy of Post-Truth." INSS Insight 1498. https://www.inss.org.il/publication/philosophy-of-post-truth/.
Jauss, Hans Robert. 1982. Toward an Aesthetic of Reception. Minneapolis: University of Minnesota Press.
Kaprow, Allan. 1993. Essays on the Blurring of Art and Life. Berkeley: University of California Press.
Khlebnikov, Velimir, and Aleksei Kruchenykh. 1913. "A Slap in the Face of Public Taste."
Kwon, Miwon. 2002. One Place After Another. Cambridge, MA: MIT Press.
Lakoff, George, and Mark Johnson. 1980. Metaphors We Live By. Chicago: University of Chicago Press. Latour, Bruno. 2017. Facing Gaia. Cambridge: Polity.
Lawson, Laura. 2023. "The Living Process of Conserving Performance." In Proceedings in Conservation and Documentation. Springer.
Lefebvre, Henri. 1991. The Production of Space. Oxford: Blackwell.
Mallarmé, Stéphane. 1897. "Un coup de dés jamais n'abolira le hasard." Cosmopolis.
Marker, Chris. 1962. La Jetée. Paris: Argos Films.
Mayakovsky, Vladimir. 1920. About This.
McKenzie, Vahri, Denise Thwaites, and Cathy Hope. 2023. "Careful and Curious: A Transformative Ethos for Artistic Evaluation." Performance Paradigm 18 (1): 128–148. McNeill, David. 1992. Hand and Mind. Chicago: University of Chicago Press.
Meersman, Philip. 2015. Visuele poëzie: Historische sleutelfiguren uit Vlaanderen binnen een internationale context (master's thesis), Vrije Universiteit Brussel, Faculteit Letteren en Wijsbegeerte
———. 2023–24. The Color of Language – The Language of Color. Research proposal, MAXLab, AP University College Antwerp.
———. 2024. The Prosody of Visual-Verbal Artefacts in Performance. Presentation, Royal
Academy of Fine Arts Antwerp and University of Antwerp, December 7.
Merleau-Ponty, Maurice. 1962. Phenomenology of Perception. London: Routledge.
Milgram, Paul, and Fumio Kishino. 1994. "A Taxonomy of Mixed Reality Visual Displays." IEICE Transactions E77-D (12): 1321–29.
Navarro Fuentes, Carlos Alberto. 2020. "Post-Truth, Media and Power: A Problem for the
Humanities." Comunicacion y Hombre: Revista Interdisciplinar de Ciencias Sociales y

Humanidades 16: 1–12. https://comunicacionyhombre.com/en/article/post-truth-media-and-
power-a-problem-for-the-humanities1-2/.
Obermeier, Christian, et al. 2013. "A Prosodic Basis for the Aesthetic Experience of Poetry." Frontiers in Psychology 4 (10): 10. Oxford Languages. 2016. "Post-Truth." Oxford Dictionaries Word of the Year 2016.
Oxford University Press. https://languages.oup.com/word-of-the-year/2016/.
Oxford Research Encyclopedia of Communication. 2018. "Post-Truth Politics and Communication." Oxford Research Encyclopedias: Communication.
Oxford University Press. https://oxfordre.com/communication/display/10.1093/acrefore/9780190228613.001.0001/acrefore-9780190228613-e-757.
Picard, Rosalind. 1997. Affective Computing. Cambridge, MA: MIT Press.
Ramachandran, V. S., and William Hirstein. 1999. "The Science of Art: A Neurological Theory of Aesthetic Experience." Journal of Consciousness Studies 6 (6–7): 15–51.
Resnais, Alain. 1961. Last Year at Marienbad. Paris: Cocinor. ScienceDirect Topics. 2020. "Post-Truth: Overview of Definitions and Theories." ScienceDirect Topics in Social Sciences.Elsevier. https://www.sciencedirect.com/topics/social-sciences/post-truth.
Schechner, Richard. 2002. Performance Studies: An Introduction. 2nd ed. New York: Routledge.
Shklovsky, Viktor. 1917. "Art as Technique." In Russian Formalist Criticism, 3–24. Lincoln: University of Nebraska Press.
Slater, Mel. 2018. "Immersion and the Illusion of Presence in Virtual Reality." British Journal of Psychology 109 (3): 431–33.
Solt, Mary Ellen, ed. 1970. Concrete Poetry: A World View. Bloomington: Indiana University Press.
Tate. 2022. "Documentation Tool: Performance Specification." London: Tate. ———. Performance Documentation and Conservation Guidelines. London: Tate Modern. https://www.tate.org.uk/about-us/projects/documentation-conservation-performance.
Tomashevsky, Boris. 1925. "Thematics." In Russian Formalist Criticism. Lincoln: University of Nebraska Press.
Tschichold, Jan. 1928. Die neue Typographie. Berlin: Bildungsverband.
Wassiliwizky, E., et al. (2017). The Emotional Power of Poetry: Neural Circuitry, Psychophysiology, Compositional Principles. Social Cognitive and Affective Neuroscience.
Zeki, Semir. 1999. Inner Vision: An Exploration of Art and the Brain. Oxford: Oxford University Press.
Zeman, A. Z., Milton, F., Smith, A., & Rylance, R. (2013). By Heart: An fMRI Study of Brain Activation by Poetry and Prose. Journal of Consciousness Studies, 20(9–10), 132–158.
Zuboff, Shoshana. 2019. The Age of Surveillance Capitalism. New York: PublicAffairs.

ANNEX B: SELECTION OF VIDEO-DOCUMENTATION OF PERFORMANCES INVOLVING PHILIP MEERSMAN

#	Year	Venue/Project	Poem/Cycle/Set information	URL
1	2006	Artiestencollectief JA!	Excerpt 1 of the performance of Artiestencollectief JA! at the poetry festival "Teranova 2006", Salle Saint-Exupery, Woippy (Metz), France. Date: 24-11-2006	https://youtu.be/aJv--hKNWh0
2	2006	Collaboration with Mario Salis	Impro Performance – Si j'étais	https://youtu.be/Vx37XdrX-j_Q?si=uDeu1RV-iNHlKbKHo
3	2006	Ghent Portus Ganda Festival	Fireworks Poem Without Fireworks Feuerwerkgedichte ohne Feuerwerk by DAstrugistenDA (Philip Meersman, Sergej Birjukov, Fjorton)	https://youtu.be/joWa2fkfYK4
4	2006	M HKA Antwerp	Benzin Gedicht	https://youtu.be/3jthonjUtCs
5	2006	M HKA Antwerp	TryOutDef Poetry Performance Philip Meersman & Fjorton	https://youtu.be/ESzVbkgeiuo
6	2008	BxlBravo Festival – Beursschouwburg	DAstrugistenDA Guantanamo Protest (Philip Meersman, Peter Waugh, Fjorton)	https://youtu.be/em4cUgfSheo
7	2008	BxlBravo Festival – Beursschouwburg	Nachtelijke Optocht from Paul van Ostaijen part of Bezette Stad Performance by DAstrugistenDA (Philip Meersman, Fjorton, Peter Waugh) Video 2022: Philip Meersman, using freely available pictures and movies online combined with the audio	https://youtu.be/MUbrmEZadUE?si=OF3GEkpWAcARZtWT
8	2008	XVI Rosario International Poetry Festival (Argentina)	Manifesto del poesia XVI at a workshop in CMD Sur Rosa Ziperovich	https://youtu.be/pnb1R4gq4u4
9	2010	Breda BUTFF Festival	DAstrugistenDA Breakfast Performance Dein Dein (Philip Meersman, Fjorton)	https://youtu.be/mjmiWpVqdV8

10	2010	Breda BUTFF Festival	DAstrugistenDA Interview with fragments of different parts of the Boxing Ring I & II Performance Series (Philip Meersman, Peter Waugh, Sergej Birjukov, Fjorton)	https://youtu.be/-BzQEzTZ9qE
11	2010	Tartu / Tallinn (Estonia)	Suur Prõmm	https://youtu.be/qxZNVVH3mqc
12	2012	Antwerp – De Groene Waterman	Boetedoening (procession)	https://youtu.be/VaWI8bfcPs0
13	2013	KASKA Performance Festival	Battlefield Poetry, a Manifesto	https://youtu.be/AMwYDO-x2d0
14	2017	Cro§in'X Collective	Cross-disciplinary Set	https://youtu.be/yYMRq9nmjrs
15	2017	Kritya International Poetry Festival (India)	At Mar Ivonios college Trivandrum	https://youtu.be/jz _ BXC6-9Mk
16	2017	Sint-Niklaas	Impro with Jean Demey Trio	https://youtu.be/g8EThttOgp8
17	2018	Mexico City	Slam MX workshop & performance	https://youtu.be/-DEe7X-52RoE?si=3bE3XT-09sAIzgUSb&t=135
18	2018	Poetry Africa, Durban – Centre for Creative Arts	Poetry Africa Festival	https://youtu.be/6gkgsLaE-fE
19	2020	Collaboration with Matete Motsoaledi	E Bonwe Ke Mang (Tears of an Orphan) (feat. Philip Meersman) · Matete Motsoaledi · Philip Meersman	https://youtu.be/iYyi9ge71IA?si=B-CBGIJM4b-pys75 _ a
20	2020	Marathon TV Host Appearance	Televised Poetry Segment	https://youtu.be/zFw3a5OcfEI
21	2021	31e Festival Internacional de Poesia de Medellin	Online poetry performance	https://www.youtube.com/live/vDBNArH-PvBM?si=brcD-gU0gYuBzLIR-B&t=1187
22	2021	Antwerp – A'pex Gallery	Frietje Wabisabi	https://youtu.be/8Dvb9Kc3CuE
23	2021	Antwerp – Winter Garden	VAXX.ON.AIR	https://youtu.be/U-hreBldZmM

24	2022	Poetrt Africa, Durban – Howard College Theatre	Poetry Picnic in the Courtyard	https://www.youtube.com/live/oppM43d _ eXw?si=zaDhju-wl _ WSZLKpf&t=9811
25	2022	Poetry Africa, Durban – Howard College Theatre	Connect the Poets / Right to Speak	https://www.youtube.com/live/JOS4E _ dIIZc?si=0RmLHXNV08FXVaCf&t=7765
26	2022	Poetry Africa, Durban – KCAP Art Centre	Drawing Resilient Future (Janna Beck coord.)	https://youtu.be/FC8-6a8pC9A
27	2022	Open Doors AP University College, Royal Academy of Fine Arts - Conservatory of Antwerp.	Red River: Philip Meersman performs as two-headed horse This performance happened in Mozilla Hubs	https://youtu.be/62AH5ANdpI8?si=oMqg1MpWqsmhsnfu
28	2024	Bright Brussels Festival	The poem 'Helder/Bright" by Philip Meersman, as part of the installation 'Beacon of Hope" by Graig Morrison. Audio recording of voices by students of the Lycée Emile Jacqmain, Brussels	https://youtu.be/Plyr6J _ BTNY?si=9cRoWHAAlpYzkXoJ
29	2024	Ohrid, North Macedonia	Ohrid Old Library Poetry Projection Performance	https://youtu.be/qKjPFROuop8
30	2024	Performance Poetry Biennial Symposium, Thessaloniki	Unfolding The Stressless Syllable	https://youtu.be/JrBEiFPf0bY
31	2024	Urban Travel Machines - A Coruna	Performer: Philip Meersman Text: improvisation based on two poems, Manifesto XVI and OPUS I Video: Hans van Rompaey Venue: Planetarium A Coruna Project: Urban Travel Machines Collaboration: live drawing by students of the Royal Academy of Fine Arts Antwerp, Interactive Design under the supervision of tutor Janna Beck, coordinator of MAXlab	https://youtu.be/b7FZufbcSLU?si=6uUwVYNZnzyWm _ Y6

wandering lonely as a cloud
there is a next level black hole waiting
a shared breath of the poetic real.

Colophon

Design: Luna Moraga Garcia

ISBN: 978-93-6354-332-4

University of Antwer
ARIA | Antwerp Researc
Institute for the Arts

Art & Research

Royal Academy of Fine Arts Antwerp
Royal Conservatoire Antwerp
AP

www.ingramcontent.com/pod-product-compliance
Ingram Content Group UK Ltd.
Pitfield, Milton Keynes, MK11 3LW, UK
UKHW041317190726
13845UKWH00025B/333